<u>An Introduction to the Gothic Style Throughout Europe</u>

By

Fred Roe

British Library Cataloguing-in-Publication Data
A catalogue record for this book is available from
the British Library

A History of Furniture

Furniture is the mass noun for the movable objects intended to support various human activities, such as seating, storing, working and sleeping. Most often, at least in the present day - furniture is the product of a lengthy design process and considered a form of decorative art. In addition to furniture's functional role, it can also serve a symbolic or religious purpose, for instance in churches, temples or shrines. It can be made from many materials, including metal, plastic, and wood - using a variety of techniques, joins and decoration, reflecting the local culture from which it originated.

Furniture has been a part of the human experience since the development of non-nomadic cultures, and even before this in its crudest form. Evidence of furniture survives from the Neolithic Period and later in antiquity in the form of paintings, such as the wall Murals discovered at Pompeii; sculpture, and examples have been excavated in Egypt and found in tombs in Ghiordes, in modern-day Turkey. Perhaps one of the most interesting archaeological sites is Skara Brae, a Neolithic village located in Orkney (an archipelago in northern Scotland). The site dates from 3100–2500 BC and due to a shortage of wood in Orkney, the people of Skara Brae were forced to build with stone, a readily available material that could be worked easily and turned into household items. Each house shows a high degree of sophistication and was equipped with an extensive assortment of stone furniture, ranging from cupboards, dressers and beds to shelves, stone seats, and limpet tanks. The stone dresser was regarded as the most important item, as it symbolically faced the entrance in each house and was therefore the first item seen when entering.

The furniture of the Middle Ages was usually heavy, oak, and ornamented with carved designs. Along with the other arts, the Italian Renaissance of the fourteenth and fifteenth century marked a rebirth in design, often inspired by the Greco-Roman tradition. A similar explosion of design, and renaissance of culture in general, occurred in Northern Europe, starting in the fifteenth century. The seventeenth century, in both Southern and Northern Europe, was characterized by opulent, often gilded Baroque designs that frequently incorporated a profusion of vegetal and scrolling ornament. Starting in the eighteenth century, furniture designs began to develop more rapidly. Although there were some styles that belonged primarily to one nation, such as 'Palladianism' in Great Britain (derived from and inspired by the designs of the Venetian architect Andrea Palladio) or 'Louis Quinze' in French furniture (characterised by supreme craftsmanship and the integration of the arts of cabinet-making, painting, and sculpture), others, such as 'Rococo' and 'Neoclassicism' were perpetuated throughout Western Europe.

The nineteenth century is usually defined by concurrent revival styles, including Gothic, Neoclassicism, and Roccoco. The design reforms of the late century introduced the 'Aesthetic movement' (essentially promoting the beauty of objects above any other social or political themes) and the 'Arts and Crafts movement' (An international design movement that flourished between 1860-1910, led by William Morris. It stood for traditional craftsmanship using simple form, often applying medieval, romantic or folk styles of decoration). Art Nouveau, in turn was influenced by both of these movements. This latter development was perhaps the most influential of all, inspired by natural forms and structures; evident primarily in architecture, but also the beautiful objects crafted to fill such spaces. Noted furniture designers in this style included William H. Bradley; the 'Dean of American Designers', Goerges de Feure, the Parisian designer who famously produced the theatre designs for *Le Chat Noir* cabaret, and Hermann Obrist, a German sculptor of the Jugendstil (the German branch of Art Nouveaux) movement.

The first three-quarters of the twentieth century are often seen as the march towards Modernism in furniture design. Modernism, in general, includes the activities and creations of those who felt traditional forms of art, architecture, literature, religious faith and social activities were becoming outdated in the new economic, social, and political environment of an emergent industrialized world. Art Deco, De Stijl, Bauhaus, Wiener Werkstätte, and Vienna Secession designers all worked to some degree within the Modernist idiom. Born from the Bauhaus and Art Deco/Streamline styles came the post WWII 'Mid-Century Modern' style using materials developed during the war including laminated plywood, plastics and fibreglass. Prime examples include furniture designed by George Nelson Associates, Charles and Ray Eames, Paul McCobb and Danish modern designers including Finn Juhl and Arne Jacobsen. Post-modern design, intersecting the Pop art movement, gained steam in the 1960s and 70s, promoted in the 1980s by groups such as the Italy-based Memphis movement. The latter group worked with ephemeral designs, featuring colourful decoration and asymmetrical shapes.

As is evident from this short history, the history of artistic developments is inextricably linked with the progression of furniture design. This is hardly surprising, as after all, many artists, thinkers and designers would stringently resist any artificial separation between traditional fine art and functional design. Both respond to their wider context and environment, both, perhaps in differing ways, seeking to impact on reality and society.

Today, British professional furniture makers have self organised into a strong and vibrant community, largely under the organisation 'The Worshipful Company of Furniture Makers', commonly referred to as the Furniture Makers or the Furniture Makers Company. Its motto is 'Straight and Strong'! Members of the Company come from many professions and disciplines, but the common link is that all members on joining must be engaged in or with the UK furnishing industry. Thus the work of the Company is delivered by members with wide ranging professional knowledge and skills in manufacturing, retailing, education, journalism; in fact any aspect of the industry. There are many similar organisations across the globe, as well as in the UK, all seeking to integrate and promote the valuable art that is furniture making. Education is a key factor in such endeavours, and maintaining strong links between professional practitioners, didactic colleges and the amateur maker/restorer is crucial. We hope the reader enjoys this book.

M EDIEVAL furniture down to the time of the Renaissance falls naturally into three periods: the first, Pointed, or 'Early English,' dating approximately from the commencement of the thirteenth century to the end of Henry III.'s reign, 1272 ; the second, Pointed, or 'Decorated,' dating from Edward I., 1272, to the death of Edward III., 1377; and the third, Pointed, or 'Perpendicular,' dating from the accession of Richard II., in 1377. In each of these periods the styles overlapped and intermingled, but with the Perpendicular style a curious circumstance is observable. This style continued in its purity till the reign of Henry VII., and then the French invasions across the Alps began to revive the traditions of pagan architecture from Rome. While, however, the Renaissance was superseding the Gothic tradition in the big cities and towns, it not infrequently happened that large buildings and works of debased Gothic character were being carried out side by side with the more fashionable style from Italy. Even at Oxford—that great seat of learning—the staircase of Christchurch College, leading to the great hall, erected as late as 1640, was a Gothic structure showing not a trace of classic influence. Something may be allowed for the architect's or craftsman's individual taste, but it is a singular fact that this was the first birth of such independence. Thus it might happen that stalls, chairs, chests, or other objects of furniture would be produced in one town which exhibited the very essence of the new style, whilst not ten miles off such articles were being made as though the Renaissance had never taken place. This sometimes renders it very difficult for those who are not absolute masters of the science to assign a correct date to individual examples. To understand and classify properly various styles of furniture, especially those which were made during what may be termed the Gothic period, a careful study of domestic architecture is not only an excellent preparation, but also of the greatest assistance, even to those who are skilled connoisseurs of furniture. Many of the old timber houses which have dates carved upon them show how an opinion ought not to be rashly hazarded as to their age. The overlapping of the various periods and lingering of older styles were such that buildings may be assigned to a later, or more probably to an earlier, period than that to which they actually belong, if the evidence of style alone is taken into account. Many buildings at Shrewsbury might be mentioned, for instance, where the Gothic style seems to have lingered to an unconscionably late date. The buildings at first sight appear to have been erected during the latter part of the fifteenth century, but a closer inspection, confirmed in many cases by actual dates, proves them to belong to the post-Gothic period, some being as late as the middle of the seventeenth.

One of the causes of our paucity of knowledge respecting furniture of the Middle Ages is the free, not to say fantastic, manner in which objects of domestic use were often rendered by the early artists. It is not until the latter end of the fourteenth century is reached that we can form any comprehensive idea as regards structural form from illustrations. We can trace the likeness of such fifteenth-century furniture as we possess to representations of similar pieces abundantly illustrated in manuscripts of this period. These indeed, are generally depicted with scrupulous care and fidelity, but it would be difficult to imagine actual examples corresponding with some of the extraordinary anomalies appearing in early artistic efforts. The greater accuracy of pictures in manuscripts made during the fifteenth century was due in a measure to a certain increase in the knowledge of perspective, added to which buildings and articles of furniture were undoubtedly in many cases drawn from the objects themselves. The illustrations to Froissart's 'Chronicles' in our British Museum, and the Bibliothèque Nationale at Paris, executed by a Fleming residing in France during the reign of Louis XI., are often marvellous in their minute representations of detail— witness the scene depicting the death of Count

Gaston de Foix, where the apartment of the inn, with its table and its credence perforated with Gothic designs, is rendered so faithfully that we could have no better record of the appointments of the place. It is noteworthy that these illustrations, as was invariably the case with medieval pictures, represented the fashions and customs of the age in which they were produced, and not those of Froissart's time. As regards English pictorial art, Lydgate's 'Life of St. Edmund,' also in the British Museum, contains several remarkable illustrations, one of which, the well-known 'Birth of St. Edmund,' is quite astonishing in its representations of bedroom furniture and appointments of the period. This picture is frequently cited as an authority.

It cannot be too strongly insisted upon that the costume of the figures which appear on buildings, as well as on chests and other articles of furniture, affords most valuable evidence of the actual date of production. Unfortunately, in England we have no furniture dating from an earlier period than the latter part of the fourteenth century on which carved figures appear, while specimens of later date are very scarce.* The tilting coffers, mentioned in Chapter VII., with their display of armour, costume, and accessories, constitute most

---

* This, of course, does not include church fittings, amongst which a few instances may perhaps be found.

A very early box exhibiting tilting knights, carved in small oblong compartments, has, I am informed, been recently discovered in the outhouse of an old garden. This relic is said to date from the end of the thirteenth century.

valuable evidences of the secular form of decoration practised at the latter end of the fourteenth century, but the number of such pieces in this country is unfortunately so limited that the record is woefully incomplete. A very remarkable painted coffer exists in Newport Church, Essex, which is more fully described later on, but in this particular instance the date is supplied by the architectural style, the figures being merely monkish portrayals of the evangelists in conventional costume.

To return to the Gothic styles. In chests the earliest carved decoration is almost invariably incised, the tracery very rarely being in relief. This, however, was not the case with other articles of furniture, for we find that the earliest chairs and tables that we possess are elaborately carved with mouldings and tracery in relief. There seems to have been a strange recurrent fashion or predilection for Scandinavian designs, for we find English coffers of the thirteenth century decorated with curious whorls or roundels filled with geometrical patterns in the Scandinavian style ; and this taste cropped up again both in the fifteenth and seventeenth centuries. It is strange that this liking for Northern design should have manifested itself at various times after the lapse of equal periods of 200 years. The geometrical patterns in these three several periods are identical, and it is only by a study of the construction of the article which they decorate that their proper dates can be ascertained.

One of the great beauties of the Gothic, or Pointed,

styles is that two pieces were very seldom made alike. Each reproduction was a separate work, like a master-piece of architecture or painting, exhibiting the producer's individuality, and was very rarely repeated without some appreciable variation. In later periods—the Jacobean, for instance, furniture of a set type was turned out by the hundred, though not so plentifully as would be the case nowadays. But with the earlier styles each piece was more or less unique. An instance can be found, however, in which three Gothic chests of late fourteenth-century workmanship, and of the very finest character, are identical in their design and treat-ment. These are to be seen at Faversham, Rainham, and St. John's Hospital, Canterbury, and are no doubt the work of some Kentish cofferer or cabinet-maker of the period. I could instance many other examples in which the designs have a great similarity, but it is seldom indeed that a case of such close identity can be discovered as that observable in these three Kentish chests.

Many of the early Gothic chests and armories were destitute of carving, but were nevertheless decorated with a profusion of scroll work in iron, which served the double purpose of strengthening and beautifying the object to which it was applied. A chest in the Victoria and Albert Museum is a fine example of this type, and a very similar specimen in much better preservation — indeed, remaining in a most perfect state—is in the Hôtel Carnavalet in Paris.

Although in such a treatise as this one cannot enter

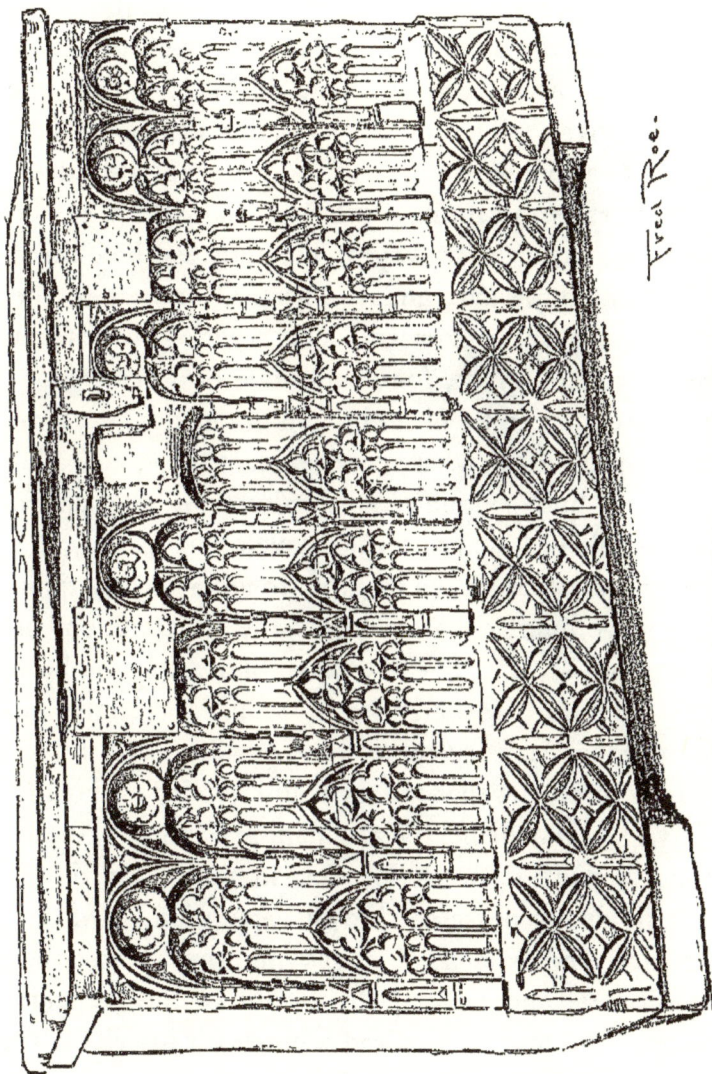

Fred Roe.

FOURTEENTH-CENTURY COFFER IN FAVERSHAM CH'RCH, KENT

One of the earliest buttressed coffers remaining in England

into a long description of the three periods of English Gothic, some acquaintance with the principles of the Gothic Pointed styles of architecture is absolutely necessary for the student before he can even conjecture the date of any piece of furniture made before the classic revival. The three principles which are best and most easily learned are : the lancet-shaped windows of the thirteenth century, or Early English style ; the flowing geometrical tracery of the fourteenth century, or Decorated period ; and the vertical tracery of the fifteenth century, or Perpendicular style. This is but a mere skeleton guide, for a multitude of other characteristics require to be filled in, and it must always be remembered that, whereas the decoration of the sumptuous and magnificent furniture of the upper classes followed closely the developments of the architectural style in vogue, the rougher productions of the more humble class clung to the old traditions of the previous style. The craftsman of repute, the best of his class in the early days, would probably be employed by rich customers to produce the finest specimen of his art that money could obtain. Though we have no knowledge of the names of any of these craftsmen, there is no doubt that in their own times they individually possessed a wide reputation. On the other hand, the expense of employing them would be proportionate, and beyond the means of the yeoman or farmer who merely required a hutch for his victuals. These worthies would be satisfied with the work of the local carpenter, who was probably a good deal behind the times, both in the matter of decorative design and in its execution.

In the first two styles of Gothic architecture we possess scarcely any specimens at all of domestic art, a few examples of chairs or benches which will be duly noticed in their proper chapter being only fragments of ecclesiastical fittings. These examples are so excessively scarce that it rarely falls to the collector's lot to acquire a specimen. Indeed, Gothic furniture is now so scarce in England that it seldom comes into the market. This is sometimes the connoisseur's chance, for dealers have hardly yet learned to appreciate such rarities properly, while the number of collectors who possess expert knowledge and appreciation of Gothic furniture may perhaps be counted on the fingers of the two hands. This may be attributed in some measure to the remoteness of the possibility of acquiring it.

Early furniture in England was constructed in a very solid and weighty fashion, as we know from the numerous coffers which abound in churches throughout the kingdom. We believe, from what we know of French furniture of the thirteenth century, that it followed on almost identical lines to similar pieces made in England. A century or so later, however, marked differences manifested themselves in the respective national methods of construction, the English developing a purely original form of decoration, and still adhering to their old heavy material and joinery, while the French and Flemish, whose elaborate flamboyant was in great measure only a reflex of the Decorated style of England, improved their methods of construction so vastly that the whole character of their furniture acquired a lightness we seldom find in English work of the period. The few examples of furniture for domestic use which remain to us of English work of the fifteenth century depend mainly for beauty upon the charming effect of their structural lines and the simplicity of their workmanship, rather than upon any surface decoration in the shape of carving. It may be this simplicity which has led to the destruction of similar pieces by the ignorant, while less pure and over-decorated specimens of a later time have been preserved. The common mind tends to associate value and beauty with an excess of frills and trimmings, and this may account for the excessive rarity of pre-Reformation domestic furniture. What the large cupboards of the fifteenth century were like may be learned from a solitary armory which remains in York Cathedral. The top is battlemented, the hinges are strap-shaped, and the arrangement of doors or shutters is very irregular. This irregularity is a distinctive and very pleasing feature of Gothic work, and is in itself an evidence of higher imaginative capacity than goes to produce an object of that absolute regularity of design which would seem to have been a weakness of later periods.

Another reason may perhaps be advanced to account for the exceptional rarity of articles of the fifteenth century. Nearly all of the second half of that period was occupied by the English people in internecine warfare of a most sanguinary character, which destroyed in a great measure the arts of peace. Between the first battle of St. Albans and the conflict on Bosworth Field some fourteen pitched battles were fought, exclusive of smaller frays and petty skirmishes, and it is probable that the number of those who actually perished in the larger conflicts alone is rather over than under 100,000. Not only was it the bone and muscle of England that was decimated ; there probably never was another war fought where so many of the wealthy nobility fell. Contrary to the usual custom of the Middle Ages, on many occasions the winning side received orders to spare the common soldiers, but slay the leaders, and those who escaped were for the most part irreparably ruined. Thus, the dissolution of great fortunes and estates impoverished the very class best able to afford the luxuries of existence. These several causes had their effect upon production. It is true that many handicrafts were still carried on with patient industry, but even these were affected by the tremendous conflict which raged throughout the country, and manufactures languished. This no doubt is the real cause why such a poverty of furniture typical of fifteenth-century work is to be found in England at the present day, compared with that of other periods, and the greater number of remaining specimens emanate from conventional sources.

At the conclusion of the wars, while England lay exhausted from her internal struggle, Flemish aptitude for business discovered in our shores an opening for Flemish wares, and articles of furniture, especially chests, were imported in such numbers that our craftsmen could make no headway against the competition, and Acts were accordingly passed at various times to restrict the importation. Whether these Acts fulfilled their purpose or not, it cannot be denied that an immense quantity of Flemish work must have been imported. In different parts of the country, even as far as the extreme West of England, we find chests still existing of flamboyant design and foreign workmanship, while old records frequently mention these by the name of Flanders chests, much in the same way as modern inventories would include Turkey carpets. Some of these Flemish chests may have been made in England by Flemish workmen from their own designs, and would still, notwithstanding this, be correctly designated as Flanders chests. It will be seen, therefore, how necessary it is to have a proper acquaintance with architectural styles in order to be able to assign to any given piece of furniture its true source and approximate date. Were the importance of this kind of knowledge duly recognised, there would be fewer errors in descriptions of Gothic and Renaissance furniture.

In treating of the decoration of early furniture, we frequently find that a conventional form of rose is introduced, and this, representing as it does the national emblem of England, has passed through so many types that a few words on it may be interesting to the connoisseur.

The earliest type of rose, which we find upon coffers as far back as the thirteenth century, seems to have been formed by a succession of concentric rings divided up by notches into petals in rather an aimless manner. In later Gothic times, however, some significance may be found in the more thoughtfully-developed form of the flower. It has been asserted, and with some show of truth, that the roses produced during the reigns of Henry V., VI., VII., and VIII. exhibit a number of petals corresponding with the distinguishing number of the reigning monarch. This is an interesting, but by no means an infallible, distinction. I have examined roses carved on buildings and pieces of furniture throughout the whole of the 150 years covered by the reigns of the monarchs referred to ; and though in some cases the theory is supported by the number of petals on the rose, in others no correspondence exists.* The favourite form seems to

ROSE FROM MISERERE SEAT, AYLESBURY CHURCH, BUCKS

* The roses on the real and sovereign of Henry VII. do not possess more than five petals each, and other instances exist which tend to disprove this theory. The four-petalled rose is seldom depicted.

have possessed an uneven number of petals, thus presenting an irregularity of scheme dear to the hearts of the early designers.

The use of the rose in decoration was common throughout England during the latter part of the fifteenth century, and there is little doubt from traces which we find that these roses were coloured, probably in accordance with the political opinions of the families who owned them. When the parties were united in the persons of Henry VII. and Elizabeth of York, both colours were variously used on the same flower, sometimes one ring of petals in red enclosing another ring in white, or *vice versâ*; or, again, as in the case of the badges exhibited in the windows of King's College Chapel, Cambridge, the rose was divided by a vertical line, one division being coloured white and the other red. The marguerite, or daisy, was also used in decoration, occasionally as a punning rebus upon the name of Margaret of Anjou, Henry VII.'s Queen.

It is to be hoped that the collector may happen to come across some of the good things bearing the badges or decorations we have mentioned in this chapter. If he does we can sincerely wish him joy, for they are excessively rare.

The decadence of the Gothic style gave birth to two features which require special mention. These were the fluted pattern popularly known as the linen panel, and the peculiar combination of scrolls which has been termed by the French *parchemin*. In my volume on

'Ancient Coffers and Cupboards' I have dealt fully with the first form of decoration, and have endeavoured to trace its origin. Briefly, I may here say that this pattern originated in France, where we find indications of it as early as about 1460. The meaning of this decoration, if it ever had any, is now lost in obscurity. The theory that it was merely used as a symbol to indicate the contents of a receptacle is now an exploded one, for some of the earliest manuscript paintings in which it is depicted represent the linen panel as appearing on the sides of pulpits and other pieces of furniture which could not possibly have been used to contain linen.

At the time of writing a linen-panelled pulpit, a most beautiful specimen of late fifteenth or early

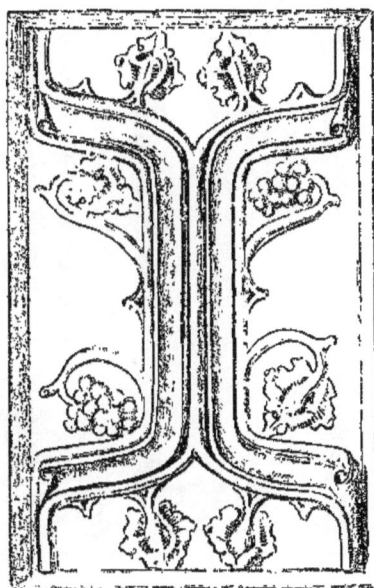

PARCHEMIN PANEL, END OF FIFTEENTH CENTURY

sixteenth century work, which for many years was hidden in one of the recesses of Henry VII.'s Chapel at Westminster, has been brought to light and re-instated in its place in the nave. It is said that Archbishop Cranmer preached from this pulpit at both the coronation and funeral of Edward VI. Probably the earliest linen panels which we possess in England are those which adorn the beautiful oak screens separating the chapels from the ambulatory on the north side of the choir of Lincoln Cathedral. These screens are locally said to have been erected during the early part of the fifteenth century, but this is no doubt an error. They can, however, hardly be of a later date than the early part of Henry VII.'s reign, as the purity of the Perpendicular Gothic tracery in the same screens demonstrates.

Although the Flemish and German types of linen panelling are usually more ornate and fanciful, some of the examples of British origin are of singularly rich design. Some of the finest English panelling of this description can be seen at Abington Abbey, near Northampton; D'Arcy Hall, Tolleshunt D'Arcy, Essex; Crowhurst Place, Surrey; The Vyne, Basingstoke; and a few fragmentary but

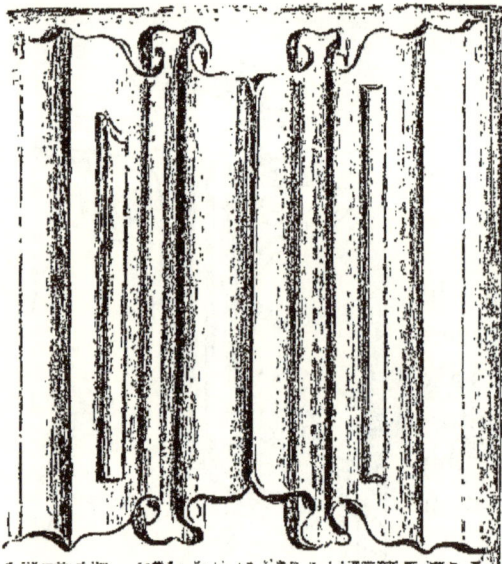

Fred Roe.

LINEN PANEL, FROM CUPBOARD REPUTED TO HAVE COME FROM PLESSIS LES TOURS

In the possession of Guy F. Laking, Esq., M.V.O.

exceptionally beautiful specimens at Rye House, Hertfordshire. There are also some excellent examples in the Victoria and Albert Museum and Hampton Court Palace. On some of the most typically English coffers and cupboards which exhibit this decoration we find that the top and bottom of the linen fold are embellished on the centre ridge with a lightly-incised cross—evidence in itself of pre-Reformation origin. I do not pretend to say that Continental examples were not decorated in the same manner, but there is no doubt that this fashion was more in vogue in England than it was in other countries. Occasionally linen panels were further decorated by augmentations in the shape of tassels and representations of conventional fruit and flowers; but these additions may be considered as mere trimmings, in no way affecting the character of the linen fold.

We do not always find that cupboards, chests, and other pieces of furniture are panelled throughout with linen fold of one pattern. The end panels are frequently of a plainer character than those in front. It is, however, possible to find cabinets and cupboards of fifteenth-century work which have elaborate linen panels at the sides, while the doors or shutters in the front remain absolutely plain and unadorned. This at first sight may seem very singular and opposed to reason, but the true explanation of the matter is this: These plain doors were probably, when first made, covered with a coat of gesso, upon which was painted *in tempera* some religious or heraldic design. This, in the course of time, became damaged or defaced, and was at last removed, leaving the ends more ornate than the front. It is true that the linen panels themselves were occasionally painted and gilded, for specimens are known remaining in this state; but in this case the painting would be on the surface of the wood, without the intervention of gesso. Some of our church screens, such as Southwold, in Suffolk, and Harberton, Devon, afford very valuable examples of what the surface decoration of fifteenth-century furniture may have been like. This linen-fold decoration passed through a variety of beautiful forms, and its last debased successors finally disappeared about the beginning of the seventeenth century. I have several times heard it argued by superficial observers that the linen was always placed so that the folds fell vertically, and that such pieces of furniture as have the decoration placed horizontally have been made up at a later period. I have only to refer those who hold this theory to the original drawing by Holbein of the More family in Basle Museum. In this the lobby is depicted as having linen panels placed horizontally, while the sideboard in the same room has them placed vertically.

Of the *parchemin* panel, the theory of evolution suggests the origin. It may be, in some measure, a late outcome of such tracery as appears in the porch of Aldham Church, Essex, or it may have been brought about by the lettered scrolls held by saints and other figures employed in ecclesiastical art. The appellation obviously suggests the possibility of this.

18

The beautiful scroll forms which it adopts are embellished more or less with cusping and conventional floral decoration. The adjacent borders of the scrolls are occasionally made to intertwine—a detail more usually observable on Flemish and German examples, but which may be seen in its very finest form on a typically English room full of panelling, in Abington Hall, near Northampton. Thoresby College, at King's Lynn, Norfolk, still possesses its original great door—a fine, massive piece of work, decorated with *parchemin* panels, and it is worth mentioning that this edifice, though actually in course of construction, was not finished in 1510, as the will of Thomas Thoresby, its founder, shows.

It is curious and worthy of notice that the linen and *parchemin* forms of decoration, although purely Gothic, did not make their appearance until the Gothic *régime* was coming to an end.

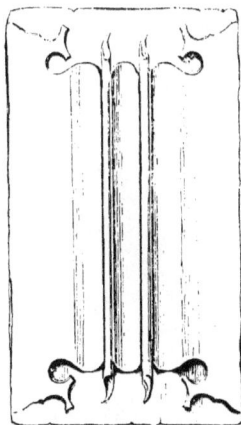

LINEN PANEL, HAMPTON COURT